A Scream Without An Echo

Manasa keerthi

Made with ❤ on the BookLeaf Publishing Platform
www.bookleafpub.in
www.bookleafpub.com

Dedication

for myself, for those who stayed, and for those who didn't

Preface

To anyone who relates. You will be okay.hold on

Acknowledgements

I have never been someone who writes.
These are words I once resented, but somehow they
found their way into poetry.
I am not a greater writer, I just write to feel seen

Thank you to the people who read what I
wrote,supported me and gently corrected my mistakes.
You helped these words turn into pages.

1. Weighted hug

And when it all comes back to you
the way darkness wraps around you like a blanket,
and you cannot let it go because it's more comfortable
than happiness now.
It leaves your mind to suffer
under the weight of things you wish would vanish
the despondence fades only the resentment stays.

2. To Liam Payne

I went numb when the news reached me,
convincing myself it was merely another prank
but then I saw you lying still
and my heart shattered into countless fragments pieces
and couldn't mended with snap of a finger
in my despair i clung to hope whispering to myself that
you were still alive, until I saw your coffin being carried
away
brought me crashing down once more
if there was one soul capable of lifting me it was you
for when death calls for me and you would be the one
welcoming
i would gladly leave my last breath
if bringing you back to life even at cost of our own lives
the Directioners wouldn't hold back

3. Coffee by the window

I sat by the window drenched from the rain
I get a coffee and a warm brownie
I looked around at people, busy in their own worlds
I wonder how many of them are connected.
Is it possible they are here just like me - ravenous for life
are they sitting here because it is raining outside and
their thoughts seem to be loud than the thunderstorms
I take a sip of coffee and think how many must have had
their first date, the beginning of a new friendship, got an
offer letter from a company and had their goodbyes
as I take the last sip of coffee and set the empty plate
aside
I wonder is anyone craving for a hug or pack their bags
and begin a new life?
I wonder if I am connected to anyone.

4. Solitude vs Solitary

Once it was a choice, now it feels like a sentence
I suddenly found myself pushed into a pit, and they gave
me ropes, but I chose the wrong ones.
I feel disgusted when I get envious,
but lately, it is the only thing I feel.
I see people laughing while my throat burns from
holding back tears.
The solitude of missing out yet the ache of being solitary
A voice whispers, *why would they care?*
another voice clamor: *it is okay you know this feeling*
has been familiar since you were a kid
Maybe someday,
I will shed this solitary blanket and simply rest in the
quiet tranquility of solitude.

5. Ugh,Stop the excuse man

You say it happens to everyone
I say..maybe not to everyone.
You say it's character-building—
I say it's suffering.
You romanticize the concept:
"It's everyone's first time living."
I say,
"It's mine too... but would I do that?"
You say it's noble to speak,
I say,
"Don't be so naïve."
You say you're just honest and straightforward
I say,
"You don't have manners."
You say it's attention.
I say,
"It's what happens when no one listens
You say,
"It's okay,"
I say
"stop the excuse man."

6. You promised, didn't you?

You gave me your words,
 and I trusted you like a fool.
It's my fault—
 I should have known better.
 But how could I?
 I was just a child.
Each time I asked, *"When do we go home?"*
 You replied, *"Someday soon."*
Ages passed.
 I asked again, *"When do we go home?"*
 And you said,
"That is not your home anymore."
Each time, again, like a fool, I asked,
"When is the next time?"
 Forgetting what your answer would be.
 Still, I asked—
 only to be shut down by your words.
Have you ever wondered
 what it feels like for me?
 Have you?
You couldn't,
 because you only ever think about yourself.
It's funny,
 how it went from *home*

to just, *"Let me visit for a few days."*
You promised me,
 didn't you?
You gave me your words.
You promised me.
 Didn't you?

7. Ephemeral

My heart races.
Everyone is going in circles,
sharing their childhood memories.
I'm next.
I wonder what to say
because I barely remember anything.
They laugh at me for not recalling,
and I want to scream —
I don't remember
because I was busy hiding sharp objects
before they turned into weapons.
I learned whose footsteps it was
before I could learn to read books.
Maybe it wasn't all bad,
I gaslight myself.
But it wasn't good either,
I remind myself.
Still —
it never felt like it belonged to me.
either does now

8. Is she to blame?

They saw her reaching out,
 lending her hands to help another soul.
 They warned her,
 "Don't be so euphonious."
At first, she didn't understand.
 Why would someone say that?
 She put everyone above herself —
 until she became the carpet
 and they just wiped their feet.
She was kind to others,
 but no one taught her
 that she had to be kind to herself too.
 She wouldn't understand that anytime soon.
Later on,
 she finally saw the reason for the warnings.
 Her kindness slowly evanesced.
 She began to choose herself —
 and they called it selfish.
They reached for her hand,
 but she had tied it behind her back.
 Not out of cruelty,
 but out of exhaustion.
Now,
 they whisper that she's inhuman,

cold.

But is it her fault?

Is she trying to protect herself...

or is she really the monster they make her out to be?

9. Jammed door

Two suitcases that's all it took
Not a proper bye nor a look.
I locked the doors, oblivious then
The keys would not fit again..

10. Two sides

The same hand that holds you so firm
Is the same hand that won't reach out when you're on
the floor.
The same beautiful smile that makes your heart dance
Is the same smile that will leave you perplexed.
The arms that hug you with warmth and softness
Are the same arms that will let go.
The same voice that whispers, "I'll be there,"
Is the same voice that will call you a con artist.
It is me. It is you.
We have all been there.
It is me. It is you.
Maybe growth comes with hurt too.

11. Mirror mirror

Mirror, mirror on the wall,
 Why do you call the words you call
the words you threw at me are the same words you tell
yourself once more
but why are you rejecting me somehow
oh mirror mirror I flinch with your distance somehow

12. Fading memories

14

Only if I knew,
 I would've taken a picture.
 Only if I knew,
 I would've stayed a few days longer,
 Had one final glimpse of you.
But does it matter now?
 The walls belong to someone else,
 Replacing my memories—
 And I'm slowly forgetting
 That feeling of home.

13. Somehow it happened

15

She became the person,
 The monster nobody wants around.
 She doesn't know how it happened,
 But it was never the intention.
You check for monsters under the bed,
 Turns out, she's with you in the house.
 If she ever becomes your home,
 Would she scare you away too?
Like she does to everyone else,
 Would you understand?
 You wouldn't, 'cause she's the monster,
 People run away from.

14. Spark?

Do you think it was true?
Or was it a fib
If it was real, why did I lose it?
Is it something that can be borrowed,
Or did I just give it to someone
'Cause I needed to be grown up?
Did it ever spark,
Or was I just envisioning someone else's?
Did the spark ever leave,
Or did I just bury it in me?

15. Flame

17

Don't blame the candle, you lit the flame.

16. What matters

Life is a long run,
 Some chase things, others just stay.
 It's a rush, never knowing where to begin,
 Nor where it will all complete.
But when it's all said and done,
 Does it really matter in the end?

17. What if

What if it wasn't true
What if we aren't fighting the same battle
What if it's in the same direction
What if everyone had equal amount of money
What if the only bruises were from playing
What if it's better, but not less
What if *what if* became *what is*

18. Hush

20

The silence between friends once echoed with laughs,
Now it stays still, words unsaid.
But memories wave in the quiet,
As our hands slowly lose each other's touch.

19. In between

21

What once was love, now is pain,
The mirror once reflected with care,
Now it shows nothing but foolishness.
Won the race, just to lose the marathon—
A muddled balance between what's gone
And a prayer that it would all come back

20. Crawl

A storm within a happy face,
 seen—
 the thoughts taking over,
 leaving the hands shaking.
the silence.
 the zoning out.
 the overstimulation.
 yet it all takes place
 in the chaos around.
when others think
 it's just mundane—
 how do you and I explain?
can we?
 'cause it's been normalized for us.

21. No echo

A scream so deafening,
It mangled the silence, yet didn't echo.